NOV 2 8 2013

AIKIDO

Alix Wood

PowerKiDS
press

New York

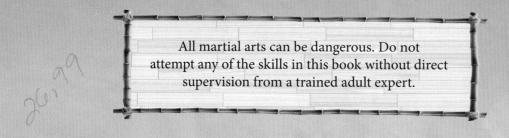

All martial arts can be dangerous. Do not attempt any of the skills in this book without direct supervision from a trained adult expert.

Published in 2013 by The Rosen Publishing Group, Inc.
29 East 21st Street, New York, NY 10010

Editor: Sara Antill
Designer: Alix Wood
Consultant: Sandra Beale-Ellis, National Association of Karate and Martial Art Schools (NAKMAS)

With grateful thanks to Finnian Cooling and everyone at Kernow Martial Arts; James, Joshua, and Elaine Latus, Olivia and Dereka Antonio, Solomon Brown, Ryan Fletcher, Alex Gobbitt, Hayden Hambly, Max Keeling, Joshua Nowell, Kyanna and Katie-Marie Orchard, Natasha Shear, Niamh Stephen, Chris Tanner, Jazmine Watkins, and Emily.

Photo Credits: 4, 5, 7, 8, 9 top and bottom, 12, 30 bottom © Shutterstock; 31 © Fotolia; Cover and all other images © Chris Robbins

Library of Congress Cataloging-in-Publication Data

Wood, Alix.
 Aikido / by Alix Wood.
    p. cm. — (A kid's guide to martial arts)
 Includes index.
 ISBN 978-1-4777-0315-1 (library binding) — ISBN 978-1-4777-0352-6 (pbk.) —
ISBN 978-1-4777-0353-3 (6-pack)
I. Aikido—Juvenile literature. I. Title.
 GV1114.35.W66 2013
 796.815'4—dc23

                          2012033061

Manufactured in the United States of America

CPSIA Compliance Information: Batch #: W13PK2: For Further Information contact Rosen Publishing, New York, New York at 1-800-237-9932

Contents

What Is Aikido?

Aikido is a Japanese martial art and a form of **self-defense**. It uses locks, holds, throws, and the opponent's own movements to overcome an attack. Aikido focuses on peace and **harmony** in its martial art.

Aikido moves are done by **blending** with the motion of your attacker. You redirect the force of the attack rather than hitting it head-on.

In aikido, mental training is as important as physical training. Aikido teaches the student to face **conflict** and not run away from it. Through this, an aikido student learns to face the situations of life in a useful way and not to avoid them or be afraid.

AI-KI-DO

The word "aikido" means "the way of harmony of the spirit." "Ai" means "harmony," "ki" means "spirit," and "do" means "way."

"Ki" is an important part of aikido. Ki is the circulating life energy thought to be in all things. **Meditation** *helps you concentrate on your inner energy, your breathing, and your heart rate.*

合 harmony

気 spirit

道 way

The History of Aikido

Aikido was created by Morihei Ueshiba. He is often known as "O Sensei" or "Great Teacher." He was born into a farming family, but he was quite small and weak. He liked to read and stay indoors.

Morihei Ueshiba

To get him outside, Morihei's father told him stories about his great-grandfather who was a **samurai** warrior. Morihei wanted to be like him, so he started studying martial arts. One day he tried to join the army, but he wasn't tall enough. He swung on trees to try and stretch his body so he was taller! On his next try, he got in the army. When Morihei left the army, he wanted to continue his martial arts training. His father built him a **dojo** on his farm to train in.

Morihei and his family moved to the island of Hokkaido. He met a *budo* martial arts grandmaster there. Morihei found himself no match for his teacher, so he threw himself into his training. He learned about peaceful ways to avoid conflict, too. Then Morihei set up his own martial arts school in Tokyo.

Hokkaido

JAPAN

Iwama ● ● Tokyo

Map of Japan

Aikido is born

Morihei moved to the village of Iwama and built a dojo. Iwama Is now considered the birth place of modern-day aikido. Before this move, his system had been called aikijutsu, then aiki-budo, and was still mainly a martial art rather than a spiritual path like it is today.

Aikido Equipment

To practice aikido safely you will need special clothes. It is best to buy your kit from your club to make sure you get the right type. At first, wear loose clothing like sweatpants and a T-shirt.

An aikido uniform is called a *dogi* or *gi*. Your belt is called an *obi*. The belt you wear shows your grade. Your gi should be kept clean, but, traditionally, your obi should never be washed.

As you progress and start sparring you might use protective gloves like these.

1 Place the middle of the obi on your stomach.

2 Pass each end of the obi behind you and back to the front.

3 Cross the right end over the left end.

4 Thread the same end up behind both loops.

5 Cross the left end over the right end. Thread the left end back through the hole to finish the knot.

In aikido some people wear wide pleated dark pants called *hakama* (above). Hakama are hard to fold, because of their pleats, and because their ties are tied in a special pattern (below). It is an old tradition that the highest ranking student has the responsibility to fold the teacher's hakama as a token of respect.

A folded hakama

9

The Dojo

The place where you learn aikido is called a dojo. The word "dojo" means "way place" or place where one studies the way.

An aikido instructor is called a *sensei*. A student of aikido is sometimes called an *aikidoka*. Always listen to your sensei and try hard to do as he says.

Your sensei will help you learn aikido safely.

Dojo rules

- Bow to O Sensei's picture or the front of the dojo when you enter or leave the dojo, or enter or leave the mat.
- If you arrive late, sit in *seiza* on the edge of the mat until sensei gives permission for you to enter.
- Always ask sensei for permission if you need to leave the mat.
- Remove watches, rings, and other jewelry before practice.
- Keep fingernails and toenails short.
- Don't sit with your back to the picture of O Sensei. Sit in seiza (below) or cross-legged on the mat.

You will need to do a kneeling bow for a belt presentation.

From seiza, lean forward and place both hands in front of you.

Sitting in seiza

CLEAN DOJO

Aikidoka should never think of cleaning as a chore. To do work that needs to be done is a sort of training, just like refining your aikido **technique**. Clean the mat before and after each class and leave the dojo in a state that shows respect for aikido.

Warming Up

It is important to warm up before you do aikido. Warming up stops you from pulling muscles. If you feel any pain, stop and switch to another exercise or stretch. Don't strain anything.

Side stretches

Stand with your feet placed shoulder width apart. Raise your left arm above your head and take a deep breath. Let your breath out slowly and lean to the right as far as possible. Then bend to the other side.

SLOWLY

Do your stretches slowly and gently, and only stretch as far as you are comfortable. The more you do, the more **flexible** you will become.

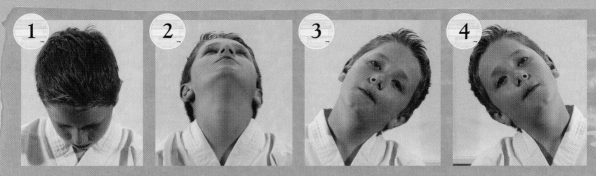

Neck stretches

Tip your head slowly forward, then back, then to the right, then to the left.

Leg stretches

Sit on the floor with your legs spread apart. Push your hands out in front of you as far as they will go.

With your knees straight, reach over and hold your left foot. Hold for a count of ten.

Swap onto your right foot and hold for a count of ten.

Stance and Arms

*A **stance** is a way of standing. The main stance in aikido is called* hanmi. *You need to keep your back straight and your head up.*

Try making your feet match the **diagram**. The red line going across is where your shoulders should be, over your feet.

Hanmi

In left hanmi the toes of your right foot turn slightly outward. The middle of your right foot should be lined up behind your left heel.

Your left shoulder is over your left hip, and your right shoulder is over your right hip.

For right hanmi, do the same but with opposite feet and shoulder position.

A well-known aikido show of strength is the "unbendable arm." It is more about posture than strength, though. You must be light on your feet, so it is easier to move you than to bend your arm. The strength needed is **core** body strength.

Unbendable arm

1 Hold your arm out straight, and tighten your arm muscles.

2 Ask a friend to put one hand on top of your elbow, and one hand under your wrist, and try to bend your arm. He should succeed.

3 Hold your arm out again, with slightly bent elbow and wrist, and relax your muscles. Use just enough muscle to hold your arm up. Look at your arm and imagine it touching something a long distance away. Have your friend try to bend your arm again. He shouldn't be able to.

Extended arms

The idea behind extended arms (right) is similar to the unbendable arm. Concentrate on extending your arms as far as possible, like trying to touch the ceiling. Remember the feeling in your arms while trying. Learning to reduce or increase the amount of energy in your arms develops great control.

15

Your Center

Aikidoka must learn to move from their tanden, or center. Your center is inside your body, just below your belly button. It is your center for balance and stability.

This rowing exercise teaches you to move from your center.

Rowing

1

Stand in hanmi and bend your knees. Breathe in as you push your hands out and move your center forward.

2

Breathe out as you bring your hands back. Bend your rear knee while bringing your center back.

Knee-walking was invented by the samurai. Samurai weren't allowed to be at the same height as the emperor. They developed knee-walking as a way of respectfully moving around. In aikido you can perform techniques while kneeling once you can knee-walk. Knee-walking will make your center strong.

DEEP BREATHING

Deep breathing helps you focus on your center. Breathe deeply in and out through your nose so your belly expands. Put your hand on your stomach to feel it rising and falling.

Knee-walking

1

Sit in seiza. Lean back, propped up on your toes.

3

Lift your left knee and push it in front of you using your hips. Always knee-walk on a soft surface, and stop if it hurts.

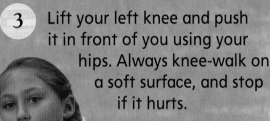

2

Lift your right knee and push it forward, moving from the hip. Keep your feet together as you walk.

17

Safe Place

One of the most important aspects of aikido is to keep yourself safe by moving out of the way of an attack. The two main methods are called irime *and* tenkan.

Both methods make you take a step toward your attacker, **pivot**, and end up safe by their side.

Irime

1	**2**	**3**	**4**
"Irime" means "entering." Stand in hanmi.	Slide your front foot forward.	Keep your feet in this position and pivot around to face the other way.	Slide your front foot back so you are in hanmi again.

Tenkan

With tenkan you lift and move one of your feet when you pivot.

"Tenkan" means "turning." Start in hanmi with your arms extended.

Keep your front foot in position. Lift the back foot and pivot around to face the other way.

Using tenkan

Stand in hanmi with your front foot the same side as the attacking hand.

Do a tenkan and pivot around to stand beside your attacker.

Falling

Aikido uses a lot of throws. You need to learn to fall safely and get back up to protect yourself as quickly as possible.

Backward fall

1 Stand in hanmi.

2 Sink down and sit with the top of your back foot touching the floor.

3 Tuck your chin into your chest and roll back.

4 Rock forward, back up onto your feet into hanmi.

5

Standing roll

It's a good idea to practice doing simple forward rolls before you try a standing roll. Stand in right hanmi. Put your right hand on the floor next to your right foot. Point your elbow forward. Push off with your back leg, and roll along your arm and along your body. Stand back in hanmi.

1

2

3

4

UKE AND NAGE

In aikido an *uke* is the receiver of a technique and the *nage* is the performer of a technique. Both are equally important in aikido practice. To be a good uke, you must learn how to fall.

Try to keep a part of your body in contact with the mat at all times. That way you roll, rather than slam, onto the mat.

Strikes and Grabs

Aikido techniques are usually a defense against an attack. To practice aikido with a partner, students must learn to deliver various types of attacks. Strikes in aikido are called atemi.

Strikes can be used to injure an attacker, or act as a distraction so you can perform another technique. In aikido, pretend strikes are sometimes used, too. The strike is never meant to hit. Your opponent must think it will, though. They duck, and let you catch them off-balance.

Head strike (*Shomenuchi*)

To strike, raise the hand that is on the same side as your back foot. Step forward and strike down at the same time. Strike down onto your opponent's forehead.

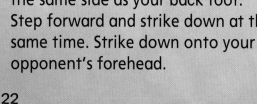

22

Chest punch (*Munetsuki*)

1

Make your hand into a fist. Your thumb should be outside your fingers.

2

Step forward with your back foot and punch with your fist. Aim for the chest or just below the ribs.

Wrist grabs

Wrist grabs allow you to stop your attacker from hurting you and disarm him if he has a weapon. They also put you in a strong position to control and unbalance him.

A same-side grab

A cross-hand grab

A double wrist grab

23

Controlling the Center

The aim of aikido is to gain control so that neither you nor your attacker are hurt. Controlling an attacker's arm or a leg is not enough. If you can control their center you can stop their attack.

Unbalancing the center (*Kokyu*)

1

Sit is seiza opposite a partner. Your partner grabs your wrists.

2

Breathe in, then as you breathe out drop your shoulders and lift your hands.

3

Turn your left hand over and push it down. Turn your whole body to the left. Your partner will lose his balance.

Basic arm pin (*ikkyo*)

1

When your opponent tries a right hand strike, get into a safe place beside her arm using irime. Stand in hanmi with your left foot forward.

2

Put your right hand on her wrist and your left hand on her elbow. As you pull her arm down, push her elbow toward her ear.

3

As she turns, lower your opponent to the floor.

4

Now you can pin your opponent's arm to the floor.

FIRST LESSON

"Ikkyo" means "first lesson." The technique needs precise timing, distance, and energy to get your attacker off balance. This is the foundation for many other techniques in aikido.

Breath Throws

Many throws in aikido are called "breath throws." Breathing out at the right time gives extra force to your throws. Also, in aikido you need to be calm under attack. Breathing patterns help you stay calm.

Breath throw 1

1 Start in hanmi.

2 As your attacker punches, do an irimi so you end up standing by her side.

3 Put your hands on her shoulders and step back with your front foot.

4 Pull back and down on your attacker's shoulders. Breathe out, bend you knees, and push her into a fall.

Breath throw 2

Use this breath throw to escape a double wrist grab. Stand in hanmi. Your attacker grabs both your wrists.

When your attacker pushes, step back with your front foot and bring your hands to your center.

Breathe out, sink down to the floor and push your hands to the outside of your back knee.

Push your arms further back and your attacker will be forced to do a forward roll.

PRACTICE

You may need to make adjustments to your technique to throw different sizes of people. If your opponent is tall you may need to bring your hands further around in step 4 to throw them. Practice makes perfect.

Terms and Symbols

Many of the words you will hear in the dojo come from Japanese. Learning some of the words and symbols is fun and will help you understand more about aikido.

Learn how to write **kanji**, the Japanese alphabet made up of symbols. The kanji on the right says "ai." "Ai" means "harmony" and is the first symbol in the word "aikido." Try following these steps to write the kanji, Use a paintbrush to get the flowing lines.

1  Paint a line from top right to bottom left.

2  Then paint a line from top left to bottom right.

3  Horizontal lines are done from left to right.

4 Vertical lines are done from top to bottom.

5  Paint this corner from left to right and then down.

6  Finish with a left to right line.

28

You may see the three shapes below in your aikido dojo. Sometimes they are drawn inside each other as one shape. The triangle symbolizes conflict, the circle represents harmony, and the square means **resolution**. They are often used as a symbol for aikido.

English	Japanese	Symbol
one	ichi	一
two	ni	二
three	san	三
four	shi	四
five	go	五
six	roku	六
seven	shichi	七
eight	hachi	八
nine	kyu	九
ten	ju	十

Words you may hear in the dojo

Japanese	How to say it	What it means
arigato gozaimasu	*ah-ree-gah-toh goh-zai-mas*	thank you very much
do itashimas'te	*doh-ee-tash-ee ma-she-tay*	you're welcome
konbon wa	*cone-bon wah*	good evening
konnichi wa	*cone-ichi-ee wah*	good afternoon
rei	*ray*	bow with respect
sensei ni rei	*sen-say nee ray*	bow to the teacher
shomen ni rei	*shoh-men nee ray*	bow to the front
yame	*yah-may*	stop
yoi	*yoy*	ready, attention

In Japanese, each syllable of a word has equal stress.

Glossary

blending (BLEND-ing)
Merging together.

conflict (KON-flikt)
A struggle or disagreement.

core (KOR)
A body's muscles that move the trunk of the body, especially the abdominals and muscles of the back.

diagram (DY-uh-gram)
A picture of something.

dojo (DOH-joh)
A training center for the martial arts.

flexible (FLEK-sih-bul)
Capable of being bent.

harmony (HAR-muh-nee)
Agreement in feeling or opinion, or a pleasing combination of elements.

kanji (KAHN-jee)
A Japanese system of writing based on borrowed or modified Chinese characters.

meditation (meh-dih-TAY-shun)
Time spent in quiet thinking.

pivot (PIHV-it)
To turn on the spot.

resolution (reh-zuh-LOO-shun)
The point at which a conflict is resolved.

samurai (SA-muh-ry)
A warrior serving a Japanese feudal lord and practicing a code of conduct which valued honor over life.

self-defense (self-dih-FENS)
Guarding oneself from an attack.

stance (STANS)
A way of standing.

technique (tek-NEEK)
A way of doing something.

Websites

Due to the changing nature of Internet links, PowerKids Press has developed an online list of websites related to the subject of this book. This site is updated regularly. Please use this link to access the list:
www.powerkidslinks.com/akgma/aiki/

Read More

Bjorklund, Ruth. *Aikido*. Martial Arts in Action. Tarrytown, NY: Marshall Cavendish Benchmark, 2011.

Crean, Susan. *Discover Japan*. Discover Countries. New York: PowerKids Press, 2012.

Santoro, Laura, and Jennifer Corso. *Aikido for Kids*. New York: Sterling Publishing, 2000.

Index